THE SEQUOIAS OF
YOSEMITE NATIONAL PARK

BY
H. THOMAS HARVEY
Professor of Ecology
San Jose State University

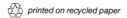

Published by the Yosemite Association
in cooperation with the National Park Service.
ISBN   0-939666-14-6

Copyright © 1978
5th Printing, 2008
Printed in China

SIZE OF
THE GIANT SEQUOIA

The giant sequoia has the distinction of being the largest living thing in the world, past or present. The individual with the record size is the General Sherman Tree in Sequoia National Park. It has a volume of about 51,000 cubic feet which, if made into a 2-by-4, would yield a board almost 175 miles long.

Through the combined attributes of rapid growth and longevity, the giant sequoia reaches its maximum height in about 800 years. If it lives on to be several thousand years old then the subsequent growth is radial. In other words, the tree adds bulk rather than height. The Grizzly Giant of Mariposa Grove, for example, is almost 16 feet in diameter at 60 feet high and over 13 feet at 120 feet above the base. The General Sherman is over 12 feet in diameter 200 feet above the base. Thus, these great columns appear as parallel structures supporting the green canopy above.

Although its close relative the coast redwood is sometimes over 50 feet taller, the giant sequoia still reaches impressive heights. The maximum height reported to date that is considered reasonable is 320 feet for a tree that subsequently had several feet knocked off its top by lightning and the resultant fire. There are, however, several living trees at 310 feet in height which are the current record holders.

The diameters of a giant sequoia vary greatly depending on how they are measured. Due to the unusually large spread of the tree's base (the butt swell) the reported values for diameters close to the ground need to be interpreted. If a ground level diameter is measured it will be greater for a tree on a slope than for that same tree on the level. Therefore, diameters taken perpendicular to the axis of the tree are preferred for comparative purposes. Diameters for forest trees are usually taken at 4.5 feet above the ground on the uphill side. This height is part of the dbh which stands for *d*iameter at *b*reast *h*eight. With large giant sequoias, however, 4.5 feet is still usually in the area of the butt swell. To circumvent this, two methods have been developed. One method selects an arbitrary height, such as ten feet, which generally places the diameter measurement above the butt swell. The other method simply takes diameter measurements above the butt swell, however far up the trunk that might be. The point of all this is that when a diameter value is given, the height above the ground must be known in order to evaluate the measurement.

The maximum diameter reported for the giant sequoia is 35.7 feet at ground level for the Boole Tree in the Converse Basin. The Grizzly Giant is not far behind at 30.7 feet at ground level. Both trees are on nearly flat ground, especially the Grizzly Giant. When measurements are taken 20 feet above the base, and thus well above the butt swell, maximum diameters are about 20 feet. Diameters of the largest trees taken at 4.5 feet above the base are from 25 to 29 feet in diameter.

Even the branches of several of the large giant sequoias are remarkable for their size. The Grizzly Giant's largest branch is 6 feet in diameter, while the General Sherman has a branch 6.8 feet in diameter and 150 feet in length. The latter branch is larger than the largest specimens of many tree species east of the Mississippi, yet, in itself, is an inconspicuous part of the tree.

These dimensions can be rattled off and some impression of the giant sequoia's size can be gained. Truly understanding such dimensions, however, is difficult. Perhaps the easiest way to comprehend a tree that is 300 feet tall and 30 feet across at its base is to mentally remove the tree from the forest and put it in other surroundings. Imagine for a moment that you are watching a football game. Our free-floating tree on its side will cover the field from goal line to goal line. Some of its branches will reach into the best seats 1/3 of the way up the stadium. Now let's move the tree to San Francisco, but keep it upright in its normal position. We will have to be in the restaurant in the tower 30 stories above the St. Francis Hotel lobby to look across at the snag-top of the tree. Or imagine that we have moved the upright tree into a typical residential neighborhood, perhaps right in front of your house. The tree will completely block the street, and you won't be able to see your neighbor's house across the street. If we mentally cut a cross section out of the tree's trunk and set it on its side, it will still be ten feet higher than the top of the two-story houses. Now we can put the tree back in the forest with an enlightened appreciation of its awesome size.

Base of Grizzly Giant

The Elephant's Foot

AGE OF
THE GIANT SEQUOIA

A reasonably close estimate of of a tree's age can be obtained by counting its growth rings. These rings are usually yearly, although sometimes rings fail to encircle the entire tree and therfore counts made of the rings may differ slightly from one radius to the next. In addition, an estimate has to be made of how long it took the tree to reach the height on its trunk where the count is being made. Given these types of variables, it is understandable why age determinations are only estimates, albeit good ones.

The annual rings are apparent in both a recently cut stump or a core removed from an intact trunk with an instrument known as an increment borer. The ring counts made on a stump are the mose reliable, for variations in growth rate during the tree's early years can be observed. The core removed with an increment borer, however, can be interpreted and a fairly reliable estimate made without cutting down the tree.

Both methods are based on the nature of growth of a woody tree stem in an area that has cold winters. The giant sequoia is like the majority of trees in having three distinct layers of tissue in its trunk. These consist of an outer bark, the growing and dividing cambium layer just beneath the bark, and the wood that forms the major portion of the mature tree. The cambium is a layer only a few cells thick and less than 1/32 of an inch across that divides and produces bark to the outside and wood to the inside. This activity occurs on an annual basis.

As the increased day length and warm temperatures of spring affect the tree, cell division begins in the cambium layer. The wood cells toward the center of the tree are relatively large and the walls light in color. This early wood, as it is called, has relatively thin walls and produces the least dense wood. As the summer progresses and available water diminishes, the size of the wood cells decreases. Their walls are relatively thick and their color dark brown. This late wood production is finally terminated when the growing season ends. These two bands of cells constitute an annual ring. One ring is generally easy to distinguish from another because the light porous early wood of the new year abuts the dense dark wood of the preceding year. By measuring the distance between two such abutments the amount of annual growth can be determined.

The quality of the site where the tree grows greatly affects this radial growth rate. A tree six feet in diameter growing in a good site, one with summer and fall water supply, may be only a few hundred years old; while another sequoia, also six feet in diameter, atop a dry ridge may be over 1000 years old. In general, however, giant sequoias from 100 to 800 years of age are a foot in diameter for every 100 years of age. In other words, a tree four feet in diameter will be 400 years old, one six feet in diameter 600 years of age.

Giant sequoias are not the oldest known living things but they are still among the ancient ones. To date, the bristlecone pines of the southwestern arid mountains are accepted as the oldest. Some of them live to be at least 4,600 years of age and a few may reach 5,000 years in their lifetimes. The oldest known giant sequoia is represented by a cut stump in the Converse Basin which, when the annual rings were counted, was determined to be at least 3,200 years of age. Some may live to be 4,000 years old as John Muir suggested from a count he made of a burned snag.

Young sequoia

Sequoia growth rings

Sequoia trunk section

NAMING THE GIANT SEQUOIA

The giant sequoia has been called a lot of different things. Three common names have often been used: big tree, Sierra redwood and giant sequoia. Lesser known common names include Wellingtonia, mammoth tree, and the distinctive Indian name Wawona. The latter name was best known throughout the world as the specific name of the famous tunnel tree in the Mariposa Grove. The Wawona Tree fell in the early months of 1969 but it is still an intriguing sight to see. The old specific name "gigantea" is occasionally used as a common name, but the technical or scientific name is now *Sequoiadendron giganteum*.

In contrast to the enduring nature of the tree itself, humans have debated over giving it a proper scientific name ever since its discovery. No less than 13 scientific names have been applied to this gigantic tree. Starting with *Wellingtonia gigantea* in 1853, it passed through or at least had a total of 11 other names proposed for it. The most famous scientific name was *Sequoia gigantea*. Its simplicity continues to appeal to many, and others are slow to leave it on technical grounds. However, *Sequoiadendron giganteum* is most generally accepted. Literally translated it means "the giant sequoia tree."

It is clearly in the redwood family of conifers with the coast redwood as its closest relative. Inasmuch as the coast redwood, *Sequoia sempervirens*, is also called a sequoia, the designation giant sequoia fits both the scientific name of the big tree and points to its close relationship to the coast redwood.

The name *Sequoia* was first applied to the coast redwood in 1847 by the Austrian botanist S. L. Endlicher. The term is probably a Latinized version of Sequoyah, the name of a remarkable Cherokee Indian who developed a written version of his people's language. Others contend, however, that sequoia was derived from the Latin "sequor" which means following, and could refer to the fact that the two sequoias of America are the remnants or followers of once widespread and numerous ancestors.

Se-quo-yah

Wawona Tree

COMPARISON OF
THE GIANT SEQUOIA
WITH THE COAST REDWOOD

Although the coast redwood and giant sequoia are considered to be close relatives, there are numerous differences. In general, their similiarities are: evergreen, cone-bearing, reddish fibrous bark, absence of resin cells, abundance of tannin, and reddish heartwood. The following chart expands on the similarities and differences between these two majestic trees.

Characteristic	Giant Sequoia	Coast Redwood
Size:	Mature trees 25-30' near base	Mature trees 12-18' near base
Diameter	Base diameter up to 35'	Base diameter up to 23'
Height	Up to 310'	Up to approximately 370'
Age	Oldest known 3,200 years Greatest reported age 4,000 years	Oldest known 1,400 years Greatest reported age 2,000 years
Bark	Rich cinnamon-brown color, deeply furrowed, as much as 2.5' thick at ridges, but generally 1-2' thick at base of large trees	Dull grey-red, shallowly fissured, ½ to 1 foot thick at base of trunks of large trees
Leaves	Small awl-shaped 1/10th to 1/2" long, appressed all around the stem; evergreen, falling with branchlets	Of two kinds, one resembling giant sequoia, others flat, needlelike in two rows; ever-green, falling with branchlets
Roots	Spread to 150' from base of tree, most in upper few feet of soil	Spread to 50' from base of tree, in upper few feet of soil
Burls	Few burls and when cut from tree will not grow leaves	When cut from tree will grow new leaves

Characteristic	Giant Sequoia	Coast Redwood

Reproduction and Growth

Cones	2-3" long, mature second season, may be retained green and growing for over 20 years, usually 34 scales arranged in spirals	About 1" long, mature and shed at end of first season, 14-24 scales arranged in spirals
Seeds	In two rows on scales, average 200 per cone	In one row on scales, average 60 per cone
Reproduction	Only by seeds	By seeds and by root or crown sprouts
Shade Tolerance	Young trees not tolerant of shade	Young trees moderately tolerant of shade
Neighbors	Usually in with other conifers	Often in nearly pure stands
Chromosomes	22 per body cell	66 per body cell

Cultivation and Commercial

Commercial Uses	Extensively used as an ornamental throughout temperate parts of the world	Extensively used as an ornamental throughout warmer parts of the world
	Wood brittle in old trees but equal to coast redwood in young trees. Few downed trees being utilized	Wood noted for resistance to decay, much used in home and other construction

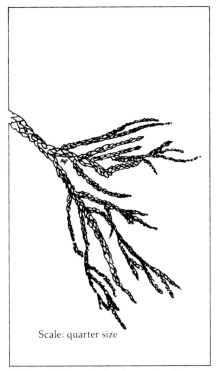

Scale: quarter size

Foliage of *Sequoiadendron giganteum*

Scale: quarter size

Foliage of *Sequoia sempervirens*

Scale: quarter size

Foliage of *Metasequoia glyptostroboides*

THE FOSSIL RECORD
AND OTHER REDWOODS

Among the conifers there is a family of trees known as Taxodiaceae, or redwoods. Once widespread throughout the world, most members have retreated to a few isolated parts of the Orient and the United States. Fifteen different species are currently recognized. Four species of the fifteen are found in the United States: the giant sequoia, the coast redwood, the southern, and the pond cypresses. The other trees of the family are mainly in China or Japan, and one interesting group is native only to Tasmania.

The redwood of China that is most closely related to the United States redwoods is called the dawn redwood *(Metasequoia glyptostroboides)*. Scientists consider it to be the closest relative of the coast redwood and, in fact, was misidentified as that for many years by paleobotanists who examined fossil specimens. The closest relative to the giant sequoia is the coast redwood, so these three tree species — giant sequoia, coast redwood and dawn redwood — are most generally accepted as "the" redwoods.

Mankind has had a most fascinating association with the dawn redwood. As implied earlier, it was first found as a fossil in the rocks and was presumed extinct. This was in 1941 when Shigeru Miki, a Japanese paleobotanist, first gave the name dawn redwood to the species. Then startling news came from China in 1946. Tsang Wang, a Chinese forester, reported that the tree was alive and well in a remote deforested valley in Szechuan Province. Excited bontanists who rushed to the scene found several healthy trees. In 1948 the famed paleobotanist Ralph Chaney brought seeds from China, and many American communities are now graced with these pleasing relics of ancient days.

The dawn redwood has several distinct characteristics that distinguish it from the coast redwood. The most outstanding feature is its deciduous habit, for each autumn its needle-like leaves turn brown and fall. The coast redwood's species name is *sempervirens* which means "evergreen." Individual leaves actually remain on the tree only three or four years, but the tree is green throughout its life. Both trees lose their leaves by having the branchlets fall rather than individual leaves.

The leaves of the dawn redwood are two ranked (a row on each side of a branchlet) and opposite one another. The leaves of the coast redwood are also two ranked, but the leaves are alternate. This distinction carries over into the cones, where the cone scales are in opposite pairs in the dawn redwood but in spirals in the coast redwood. In its native haunts the dawn redwood may reach heights of 140 feet; while the coast redwood is the tallest of all trees, approaching 370 feet in height.

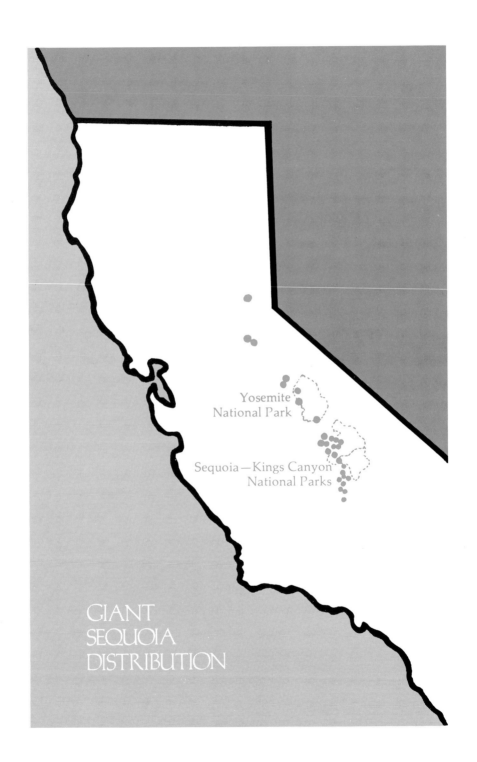

Yosemite
National Park

Sequoia—Kings Canyon
National Parks

GIANT
SEQUOIA
DISTRIBUTION

DISTRIBUTION OF THE GIANT SEQUOIA

The entire native range of the giant sequoia is an area only 250 miles long by 15 miles wide on the western slope of the Sierra Nevada of California. Primarily found at elevations between 5,000 and 7,000 feet, the lowest elevation tree grows at 2,800 feet and the highest at 8,900 feet. Seventy-five groves are recognized by name throughout the range. The most northerly, the Placer County Grove, consists of only six trees growing at an elevation of 5,250 feet. About 250 miles to the south is the Deer Creek Grove which was logged in part, but still has several large giant sequoias. Eight of the groves are in the northern 2/3 of the range and are relatively small in extent. The remaining 90% of the groves are in the southern 1/3 of the range and often contain thousands of large sequoias. The largest grove is the Redwood Mountain Grove of Kings Canyon National Park. Altogether the giant sequoia groves cover over 35,000 acres, of which over 95% is in public ownership.

The fact that the giant sequoia occurs in distinct groves, some widely separated, has intrigued people since first it was noted. What could account for this disjunct distribution? John Muir was among the first to suggest that the most recent glaciers may have divided up a once continuous belt of sequoias. Others propose that a hotter, drier period in the Sierran climate 4,000 to 5,000 years ago eliminated sequoias except for those on moister sites. And finally there is the possibility that the giant sequoias migrated over the Sierra in different places and thus gave rise to separate groves or clusters of groves on the western slope. None of these ideas excludes the others, so it may well be that all three factors have operated either together or separately or at specific parts of the range during the past.

Although some of the groves appear to be in a healthy condition and have enough young trees to replace the old ones when they die, many small groves lack adequate replacements. The factors that contribute to this situation are no doubt numerous and complex, but one common feature of these nonreproducing groves is the absence of fire. Although fire may kill most trees, the giant sequoia actually is favored by fire of the proper intensity and frequency.

GIANT SEQUOIA
ECOLOGY AND LIFE HISTORY

Ecology, the study of the interdependence of living things and their environments, yields an understanding of the giant sequoia's place in nature. Its story is one of survival in the face of disasters which would destroy other, lesser trees. This mammoth tree is faced, as are all other living things, with crucial periods in its life history. From struggling seedling to aged giant, the tree is confronted with adverse forces. The seedling just emerging from the forest floor may die aborning as it lifts its first leaves to the summer sun. Forest insects such as camel crickets or caterpillars may chew off the leaves or girdle the diminutive stem. Heat cankers may dry and kill the stem or underground molds may attack the roots. And the greatest of all destructive forces — drought — may cause the roots and leaves to wither and the young seedling will die.

Those seedlings that circumvent all the above hazards may then start a living journey that can last over 3,000 years. Up until about 400 years, however, death rates are high. Drought and other factors that adversely affected them as seedlings are still present, but shading from adjacent trees starts to take the greatest toll. Giant sequoias require abundant light. If the tree grows where less than ¼ of full sunlight falls upon it, then the young tree is in trouble. Later on, an older tree can compensate for shade. Only the lower branches will be lost on a giant with its top above the rest of the forest, and this loss of lower branches enables such a tree to withstand one of the scourges of the forest — fire.

The giant sequoia quickly grows an unusually thick bark that insulates the living tissue beneath the bark from the heat of fire. This, coupled with shade-killed branches that drop, enables older trees to withstand all but the worst holocausts. The bark on a mature sequoia is often a foot in thickness near the base of the tree, and may reach two and one-half feet on exceptional specimens. It is thick enough on trees only a hundred years old to allow them to withstand a fire that kills adjacent white fir.

Sequoia germinating

Sequoia seedling

Sequoia: approx. 75 years old

Fire, to which the giant sequoia is tolerant, also aids in the trees' reproduction. Fire sweeps the forest floor clean so that the minute seeds of the giant sequoia may come to rest on rich mineral soil where seedlings do best. Although the seeds can germinate in the fallen branches and leaves on the forest floor, the seedlings often die because any of the several factors discussed earlier are more prevalent in the organic litter. In addition to those factors, however, is the threat of disease organisms in the soil and litter in areas not cleared by fire. Particularly hot fires sterilize the soil and make it easier for young roots to penetrate quickly to life-sustaining moisture.

In order to open and shed seeds, giant sequoia cones must be completely dry. Fire causes hot drying air to rise and open up the closed sequoia cones high in the air. The resultant shower of seeds falls on a favorable seedbed prepared by the same fire. Thus, at practically all stages in its life history, the giant sequoia either tolerates or is favored by fire. It does not depend only on fire, however, for regeneration.

The giant sequoias shed seeds throughout the year which, if they fall on exposed soil, may produce new trees. One of the major factors in turning up new soil is the falling of trees. As their roots are pulled from the earth, the pit that remains provides a suitable substrate for seedling sequoias. John Muir once suggested that just the falling of giant sequoias would provide enough suitable soil for young sequoia trees. When large forests are examined for such replacement, however, there are too few seedlings in the pits to replace all the trees that have fallen; so the idea, while intriguing, is unproven.

The seeds that fall without the aid of fire come mainly from two sources. The Douglas squirrel eats the cones of pines and firs as well as sequoias. The difference is that while it eats the actual seeds of pines and firs, it prefers the fleshy cone scales of the giant sequoia cones. Though a few seeds are eaten, most fall to the ground.

The second source of seeds is due to the action of a minute beetle. This small long-horned beetle attacks the giant sequoia cones in search of food. Although it may destroy a few seeds, the beetle generally tunnels through the central axis of the cone. By so doing, the transport of water to the cone is severed and the cone dries out. As the cone dries, the cone scales separate and the seeds are set free. Inasmuch as a mature tree may add 1,500 cones a year, and there are about 200 seeds per cone, there is a tremendous seed source available for release by the action of the Douglas squirrel and this beetle.

Many other insects interact with the tree in addition to the beetle. Over 140 insect species have been found to depend directly or indirectly on the giant sequoia. They may live their entire lives on one vast branch high in the air. Most are remarkably small and are foliage colored insects, so that they escape notice. A small green aphid may occur in the tens of thousands feeding on juices in the foliage. In turn, it is fed upon by voracious larvae of the green lacewing, which fall prey to robber flies; these are consumed by flycatchers, which subsequently are eaten by hawks. Thus, the chain of life is linked from the grand food producer, the giant sequoia, to the ultimate consumer, the carnivorous hawk.

As dramatic as the predator food chain may be, it is more than offset by the slow, quiet decomposition of leaves and wood produced by the giant sequoia. Each year the leaves and twigs fall to the ground to be consumed by the unseen bacteria and fungi in the forest floor. Each year giant sequoias fall and though it may take many centuries they, too, will be consumed in the subtle process of decay, the major process of the forest.

The "shelter" tree

A MONUMENT TO SURVIVAL

The giant sequoia stands supreme among the green plants — in fact, among all living things in that it is the largest of them all. It towers above its neighbors with a quiet majesty, a majesty born of the centuries of survival when others failed. It stands with solid grandeur on dry mountain slopes and moist meadow borders. It is the first to greet the morning sunrise and the last to witness the sunset. The giant sequoia persists even though numerous forces drive it toward extinction. It survives because it has adjusted to the present adversities and holds claim on the future. A single tree in its lifetime will spill millions of seeds with the humble objective of replacing only itself. If conditions are right it will do more than that, and those who appreciate great trees will look upon these survivors and find them good.

Moss on fallen sequoia

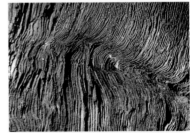

Sequoia wood pattern

Young sequoia in Valley: approx. 100 years old

Burn scar

WHAT TO SEE AND DO
IN THE MARIPOSA GROVE

The Mariposa Grove, located near the south entrance of Yosemite National Park, can be reached by travelling north on Highway 41 from Fresno or by going south on the park road from Yosemite Valley.

About two miles east of the south entrance these magnificent trees first come into view. Their rusty brown bark contrasts starkly with the dull grey of adjacent species. After parking in the lot near the entrance to the grove, you may either walk the trail — including the two posted nature trails — or ride the tram that operates during the summer months. The tram operators provide a running commentary on the grove, stopping at various viewpoints where you may disembark and walk to other points of interest in the grove. The map on page 25 shows the locations of these various points of interest and sequoias with special attributes that are described below.

(Map of grove with these trees located and tram stops shown.)

The Fallen Monarch — This tree is remarkable for it fell long ago and remained almost entirely intact. Old growth giant sequoias are noted for their brittle wood, a factor that reduced their value for lumber. In fact, the wood was generally cut into fairly small pieces, and many of the grapestakes in San Joaquin Valley vineyards are giant sequoias. The Fallen Monarch is a little over 15 feet in diameter at 10 feet above the base. The sapwood and bark have long since decayed, but were they placed back on the tree the diameter would probably be an impressive 18 feet. Giant sequoia heartwood is slow to decay, and remnants of trees measured by radio-carbon dating have yielded specimens up to 2000 years old. At varous times in the Fallen Monarch's history, stagecoaches were driven on the trunk and stairs provided access to the upper side. Walking along side this fallen giant, contemplating how long ago it once stood, is still a most impressive experience. The fir tree leaning over its upper section suggests the great tree fell at least several hundred years ago.

The Corridor Tree — This unusual specimen testifies to the endurance of the giant sequoia. Repeated fires and possible decay have eaten away at the base creating gaping holes large enough to walk through. The remaining flying buttresses show regrowth of new wood starting to fill in the gaps. The buttresses also continue to support a tree of grand proportions: almost 250 feet tall and 15 feet in diameter at 10 feet above the ground.

The Three Graces — These three well-named trees are an excellent example of the giant sequoia's capacity to grow to great size in close proximity. Frequently, groups of five to ten trees grow within 50 feet of one another. What would ordinarily be competition between individuals is resolved by cooperation. The roots of the trees fuse together and support one another rather than remain

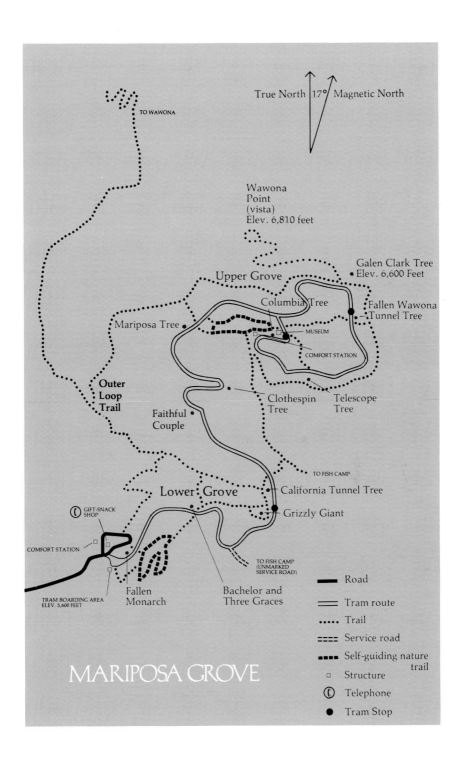

True North 17° Magnetic North

TO WAWONA

Wawona
Point
(vista)
Elev. 6,810 feet

Galen Clark Tree
• Elev. 6,600 Feet

Upper Grove

Columbia Tree

Fallen Wawona
Tunnel Tree

Mariposa Tree •

MUSEUM

COMFORT STATION

**Outer
Loop
Trail**

Clothespin
Tree

Telescope
Tree

Faithful
Couple •

TO FISH CAMP

Lower Grove

California Tunnel Tree

GIFT-SNACK
SHOP

Grizzly Giant

COMFORT STATION

TO FISH CAMP
(UNMARKED
SERVICE ROAD)

TRAM BOARDING AREA
ELEV. 5,600 FEET

Fallen
Monarch

Bachelor and
Three Graces

Road

Tram route

••••• Trail

==== Service road

▬▬▬▬ Self-guiding nature
        trail

□ Structure

ⓒ Telephone

● Tram Stop

MARIPOSA GROVE

independent. The Three Graces probably are the survivors of a once dense stand of giant sequoias that seeded in after a fire many centuries ago.

All of the Three Graces are over 200 feet all, with the tallest one nearly 260 feet in height. To see these trees highlighted by the morning sun is one of the many unexpected treats the Mariposa Grove offers.

The Grizzly Giant — This rugged tree is the largest and oldest tree in the Mariposa Grove. Although it is only a little over 200 feet tall, its massive trunk rises impressively in an almost straight column. The great column, nearly 31 feet across at the base, tapers to about 16 feet in diameter at 60 feet above the base, and is still over 13 feet across at 120 feet above ground level. The first large limb at 95 feet above the ground is 6 feet in diameter. Many of the trees near the Grizzly Giant are not equal to just this one branch.

The Grizzly Giant has endured many centuries of Sierran storms and the impact of human activity. The first roads in the area went right over the roots of the great giant. Well-meaning people employed barriers of all sorts to keep other people away from the base of the tree. They dug fence holes that severed the roots, as did holes for the shrubs planted in 1930 to conceal barbed wire strewn around the base of the trunk. Through all these indignities, the noble tree has survived and is growing well. Its estimated age is between 2,500 and 3,000 years.

The California Tree — The past propensity of people to cut tunnels through large trees is apparent in this tree. The tunnel was cut through in 1895, 14 years after the famous Wawona Tree was tunneled. When winter snows blocked the stagecoach road to the upper grove where the Wawona Tree is located, clever drivers placed the Wawona Tree sign at the California Tree. Thus, for many years it served as a substitute until the road was relocated in 1932. The old road now serves as a footpath and you can view up close the gradual healing of the great wound.

The California Tree is slightly over 230 feet tall and has a diameter of almost 15 feet at 10 feet above the ground. As with the Wawona Tree, burn scars were enlarged to make the tunnel in the California Tree. It is located about 100 yards northeast of the Grizzly Giant.

The Faithful Couple — The name Faithful Couple is an apt one for these two trees that have grown closer together through the years. Even more than the Three Graces, these trees exhibit the ability of giant sequoias to graft to one another. Though many trees in the forest can do this, the naturally great size of the giant sequoia makes it a particularly striking sight. The combined trunk is nearly 40 feet in diameter near the base and the twin columns reach almost 250 feet high.

The Mather Tree — At the bend in the road uphill from the Faithful Couple stands a relatively young giant sequoia named after Stephen T. Mather, the first Director of the National Park Service. Mather served from the establishment of the Park Service in 1916 until 1929. As a Californian, it is appropriate that he be honored with one of the California's biggest trees.

The Mather Tree is a good example of the giant sequoia's younger growth form called a spire-top. This sharply pointed outline results from the rapidly growing tip which is exceeding the lateral, spreading growth. Trees with this growth habit are identified as excurrent, while those in which all the terminal shoots grow at the same rate are called decurrent. An oak tree is a good example of the latter type, which accounts for the rounded profile of these trees. The rapid vertical growth of the giant sequoia generally assures it ample sunshine. It would soon die if forced to live too long in the shadow of other trees, for the giant sequoia cannot tolerate shade.

Mather Tree

Tram in Mariposa Grove

The Clothespin Tree — Repeated fires have consumed the base of this tree so that it resembles an old-fashioned clothespin. At 10 feet above the ground the tree is 16 feet across and it towers to almost 270 feet in the air. The gaping wound is 70 feet high and 16 feet across at the base. Although fire appears to be the major factor that created the opening, fire has not killed the tree. Even though the majority of the original connections between roots and stem have been severed, the Clothespin Tree is in apparent good health and produces cones in adequate numbers.

The Mariposa Tree — This tree is another fine specimen standing about 250 feet tall and a magnificent 17½ feet in diameter at 10 feet above the ground. Not only is the tree magnificent, but it demonstrates rather well how new growth of wood and bark gradually heal fire scars. Notice how this new growth from the sides of the tree where living tissues still survive is beginning to cover the old wound.

The tree as well as the grove was named after the famous gold rush county of Mariposa to the west of Yosemite National Park; the grove lies within Mariposa County. The county took its name from a stream that the early Spaniards had called Las Mariposas, meaning "the butterflies."

Throughout this paper we have been comparing sizes of the giant sequoias. Meaningful measurements of giant sequoia diameters, however, can be difficult to make. The difficulty arises from the inconsistency of the bulge, or butt swell, at the bases of large trees. Standard forest practice is to measure at 4½ feet, which is called the dbh (for *d*iameter at *b*reast *h*eight), but measuring large giant sequoias at breast height generally would include the butt swell. Therefore, in order to somewhat standardize diameter measurements for better comparison, Mariposa Grove diameters have been made at 10 feet above the ground.

Big Trees Lodge Area — The large relatively level area to the north of the road was the former site of the Big Trees Lodge built in 1933 to provide meals and lodgings to Park visitors. To reduce development and resource impact in the Mariposa Grove the lodge structure was razed in 1982. The presence of mineral soil, adequate sunshine and moisture on this disturbed site probably accounts for the large number of young sequoias in this area. On close inspection of their foliage, you can see and feel the sharp awl-shaped leaves. If a branch from a large tree is available, compare its leaves with those of trees just a few decades old.

The Elephant's Foot — This fallen sequoia reveals an unexpected attribute of these gigantic trees: They lack a tap root. The largest of living things stands much like a nail on its head. Shallow, widespread roots are a necessary adaptation to the thin soils of the moutains, and giant sequoia roots are usually only in the top few feet of the soil. The roots from some trees reach out over 150 feet from the base, enabling the tree to absorb adequate soil moisture for growth when it is available. When a tree falls over, it exposes this shallow disk of roots, as in the Elephant's Foot.

Grizzly Giant — winter

The Sunset Tree — Behind the Lodge stands a giant sequoia that has been battered by the elements. At its base a fire scar stretches over 50 feet of the perimeter, heavy scarring even for a giant sequoia. Such a massive severence of the water transport connections between roots and trunk causes the upper branches and leader to die, so that many old sequoias exhibit a snag-top growth form. Inevitably, fallen wood will accumulate at the base of an old tree, and when fire strikes it burns this ready fuel source especially hot.

The Sunset Tree was named because it stands on the western edge of the grove and is the last to be lit by the setting sun. Though only a little over 200 feet high, the Sunset Tree is a robust 17 feet in diameter at 10 feet above the base.

The American Legion Tree — This tree was dedicated to the unknown dead of the First World War in 1921. It is another good example of a forest veteran that has survived fire and storm and continues to put out new leaves and cones each year. A tree of fairly remarkable dimensions, it is over 18 feet in diameter at 10 feet above the mean base and 250 feet tall.

The Haverford Tree — Because the cavernous central cavity is large enough to shelter horses, in early stage coach days the tree was known as the Shelter Tree. Old reports say as many as fifteen horses found shelter during stormy weather in the almost 30 square foot cavity. At 270 feet, it is one of the taller trees in the grove and is a respectable 16½ feet in diameter at 10 feet above the ground.

The Museum — Galen Clark was so impressed with this area of the grove that he built his cabin at the present museum site in 1861. This cabin was replaced by another in 1885, which was enlarged in 1902. This structure was rebuilt in 1930 and now serves as the Park Museum for the Mariposa Grove. Exhibits inside the present Museum tell the story of the giant sequoia ecosystem. During the summer a naturalist is there to help interpret the area. Take a few minutes to sit on the porch and contemplate what it must have been like over a hundred years ago when Clark lived in this remote mountain haven with these magnificent trees in his front yard.

The General Grant Tree — Directly in front of the museum porch is a fine specimen of the giant sequoia. It bears the name of General Grant, but do not confuse it with the General Grant Tree of Kings Canyon National Park. The latter, also known as the Nation's Christmas Tree, is about 255 feet tall and has a dbh of almost 29 feet, making it the second largest giant sequoia. The General Grant Tree in Mariposa Grove is about 270 feet tall and has a diameter at 10 feet above the base of almost 14 feet. Scientists use total trunk volume to determine largeness, and while there is no figure on the Mariposa Grove General Grant, the Kings Canyon General Grant has a volume of 47,500 cubic feet.

The General Sherman Tree — To the left of the General Grant Tree is the splendid General Sherman Tree. It, too, towers to almost 270 feet and is about

13½ feet in diameter at 10 feet above ground level. Again, do not confuse this with the largest giant sequoia of all, the General Sherman Tree of Sequoia National Park. The largest tree in the world by trunk volume is 275 feet tall and has a dbh of 25 feet. Its trunk volume of nearly 51,000 cubic feet has earned it the title of the largest living thing in the world, past or present.

The Fallen Giant — This fallen giant sequoia was intact until cut in 1934 during rerouting of the road. The cut enables one to see the dark exudate that coats the cut surfaces. When oxidized the exudate changes from a reddish substance to a very dark purple. Many different chemicals are in the exudate and they serve to make the heartwood relatively resistant to decay. Eventually the chemicals break down and the wood will decay, although it may take many centuries. The sapwood, the light colored wood three to four inches thick forming an outer cylinder, is without the reddish chemicals. This wood decays rather quickly on fallen logs, sometimes within a few decades. The Fallen Giant, which toppled in 1873, has lost its sapwood to decay and only the heartwood remains.

The Columbia Tree — Looking west from the Museum beyond the Fallen Giant and to the right of the road are three giant sequoias. The largest one with an inverted V-shaped fire scar is the tallest sequoia in the grove. The Columbia tree is almost 290 feet in height and about 16½ feet in diameter at 10 feet above the ground.

In other groves, giant sequoias sometimes reach heights of 310 feet. This upper limit to growth seems due in large part to problems of water supply to the top branches. Although 50 to 60 inches of rain fall each year in the giant sequoia belt, it is essentially a rainless place during the late summer and fall. This period of drought places a stress on the upper branches, slowing their growth. Then, if fires sever root connections, some top branches will die to produce a snag-topped tree.

The Four Guardsmen — A short walk to the west of the Museum four giant sequoias stand in a row. All of them are over 200 feet in height and they are between 8½ and 10½ feet in diameter at 10 feet above the ground. How did this interesting pattern develop? There are several possible explanations for trees growing in a straight line.

In a very wet climate where fires seldom clear the forest floor, a fallen tree in the process of decay may serve as a seedbed. Such trees are called "nurse trees" as they sustain young seedlings with their decomposing trunks until the seedlings' roots reach the mineral soil. But in a relatively dry climate such as the Sierra, fire may entirely consume a fallen tree and thus prepare a linear seedbed. Seedlings of giant sequoias survive best in soils that are heated the hottest. Thus, this latter explanation perhaps best explains the Four Guardsmen as they stand at attention all in a row.

Four Guardsmen

Mariposa Grove Museum

The Fallen Utah Tree — Giant sequoias die for a variety of reasons. Some die standing while many large ones topple over. The factors that lead to their fall vary and are not always operating singly. Lack of sufficient root support is the basic problem, although a few have their trunks snap several feet above the ground. Factors involved in making insufficient root support and ultimately falling are fire scars, decayed roots, carpenter ant galleries, undercutting by streams, extreme heavy loading by snow and ice, strong winds, or a combination of several of the above. Most giant sequoias with fire scars fall toward the side with the scar. Most sequoias adjacent to wet meadows fall toward the meadow. Most sequoias fall in the winter or early spring when storms and wet soil are the final factor in their failure.

The Utah Tree fell at 7:00 a.m. on April 7, 1935, a few days after a wind storm. It fell on a calm day. We believe, however, that the storm weakened its support. Further, a wind storm tends to dry out leaves. As water was carried back to the leaves, it may have ascended unevenly creating an unbalanced upper portion.

As with many plants, even though they have not lost root connections to the soil, parts of them can remain alive. So it was with the Utah Tree that had green foliage on it three years after it fell.

The Fallen Stable Tree — This grand old tree fell to its death the year before the Utah Tree succumbed. Fire had previously destroyed the wood in much of the base so that as its name implies, it had been used as a stable. When it fell, it broke into three main sections, a common occurence with old growth giant sequoias as they are noted for their brittle wood. As with the Utah Tree, it, too, had new shoots growing two years after its fall. Though the date of falling technically may not be the date of death for a tree, unless some root connections remain intact, the tree is as good as dead.

An interesting aside is that a small (approximately two foot dbh) sequoia in the Atwell Mill Grove fell several years ago, but the roots remained connected with the stem. The living branches subsequently grew skyward and at present look like a line of minature trees.

The Fallen Massachusetts Tree — This fallen mammoth must have been a tremendous sight to see before it fell in the spring of 1927. Once it was one of the largest trees in the grove at 28 feet in diameter at 10 feet above the ground and an estimated 280 feet in height.

In addition to loss of support due to fire and decay, road construction in the 1870's had severed its roots. Then a spring storm dumped a heavy load of snow on the Massachusetts Tree and that was the final straw. In falling, it broke into many sections on hilly land.

The Telescope Tree — To understand how this tree got its name, you have to walk inside it. There you can see it has a hollowed-out center so that you can

33

look up through it and see the sky above. The processes that probably produced this phenomenon were heart rot followed by fire. Although the heartwood of a giant sequoia resists decay fairly well, the older heartwood, i.e., that nearest the center, becomes less resistant with the passage of time. Once decay had decreased the density of the central heartwood, a fire starting at the base or possibly from the top due to lightning, could burn out the center of the tree. Repeated fires probably were necessary to create the size of cavity that is now evident in the Telescope Tree. About half the basal perimeter has been destroyed by fire, but the outer shell of the tree consists of the three vital layers for any tree — the bark, the growing cambium, and the sapwood.

The Telescope Tree is only about 190 feet tall and 16½ feet in diameter at 10 feet above the ground. It probably was well over 200 feet tall before it was converted into a hollow cylinder and lost much of its top. Through it all, however, the tree survives.

The Fallen Wawona Tree (Tunnel Tree) — Undoubtedly, the most famous, widely known tree in the world is the Wawona Tree. From 1881 when the tunnel was first cut, until 1969 when it fell, hundreds of thousands of people travelled from all over the world to the tree that you could drive through. Although other sequoias have been tunneled, the Wawona Tree was preeminent. The Scribner brothers cut the tunnel in 1881 for only $75. They selected a large tree (its diameter was almost twenty feet at ten feet above ground level, and it was 235 feet tall) with large burn scars. The tunnel was 26 feet long, 8 feet wide and 10 feet high.

In the heavy winter of 1968-69, the most famous tree in the world fell, probably in part due to the massive tunnel through its base. It had survived an estimated 2,200 years. Perhaps the fact that it served to bring countless thousands to the Mariposa Grove and that perhaps in their pilgrimage they also found the deeper values of a forest of uncut giant trees, offset the tragedy of its death.

The Galen Clark Tree — Although not a particularly large giant sequoia (about 15½ feet in diameter at 10 feet above the base and 240 feet tall) the Galen Clark Tree is unusual on several counts. It is unusually free of fire scars, possibly because it is near the top of the ridge where little fuel may roll down hill and lodge against the tree. Its silvery appearance is striking. And it is likely the first tree that Galen Clark saw because he first entered the grove from the north.

It is fitting that we end this narration with the Galen Clark Tree. Galen Clark, more than anyone else, first brought people to witness the giant sequoias of the Mariposa Grove. He chose to live alone among them, and it is likely that he saw them all as individuals and grew to know them well, almost as friends. Just as the bark on the tree named in his honor is an unusual silvery color, so each tree has something unique about it. And yet each one stands in quiet dignity, sharing a special nobility that transcends even their size, the nobility of true monarchs.

Galen Clark Tree

NOTES

Design, illustrations, typography by Steven Goldberg and Associates, Yosemite National Park. PHOTOS: National Park Service, Wm. F. Dengler, Eastman Kodak Co., Steve Goldberg, Bruce Fincham, L.W. McKenzie, Fred Mang, Jr., H. Windsor, N. Messigner, Ted Orland.